MW00887336

FIGHTING THE

Pink Giant

BETSY BULLARD

Fighting the Pink Giant:

A story inspired by a battle against breast cancer.

By: Betsy Bullard
Illustration by: Breanna Smith

Stages

The Cruise Connection

Here I am getting out of the shower in a small bathroom in our cabin on the ship. I was on my first cruise with my son, sister, best friend, and her son celebrating an early 50 birthday with them in April during Spring Break. I was an elementary school assistant principal and enjoyed breaks from school and the busy 60+ hour workweeks, dealing with students, staff, buses, books, and you name it! However, we were having lots of fun eating at all hours of the day and night, playing music bingo, going to magic shows, karaoke, comedies, shops, and the Bahamas baby! The weather was beautiful, the drive down to Cape Canaveral, Florida was fun, eating cake by the ocean, and we were laughing often... just what I needed after a hard six months of losing my mother and caring for my suddenly alone 90-year-old father. But as I was standing in front of the mirror, I wondered why my left breast seemed so tender and darker looking than the other. I chalked it up to bumping into something and "at my age" not remembering what. So, I let it go. We had a birthday bash to continue! Little did I know that I was just beginning my unlikely sail on rough waters in my life. It must have been my April Fool's joke...I wasn't as healthy as I thought. Little did I know that in a few weeks, my cruise would be a distant memory of a fun get-away and the next 10 months would be a struggle on land.

Philippians 4:12-13 ~*I know what it is to be in need, and I know what it is to have plenty. I have learned the secret of being content in any and every situation, whether well fed or hungry, whether living in plenty or in want. I can do all this through him who gives me strength.*

Doctors' Appointments

When I got home from the cruise, I was more observant as to drying off and looking in the mirror at my breast. Yes, it continued to look bruised in the nipple area and a few days later I noticed a red looking "hot spot" under my breast. Of course, I chalked that up to my large breasts laying down on the folds of my skin or sweating or my bra. As I kept an eye on my left breast and did self-exams every night in the shower, I also started going online and searching for different causes for changes in breast color, tenderness, and reasons for redness. All of the search engines kept coming back to the phrase, "See your doctor." So, I made an appointment with my gynecologist, since I as overdue for a mammogram and had some other female symptoms going on that approaching-fifty-year-olds need to discuss. I told the nurse my concerns before the doctor came in the room. While getting into the paper vest and sitting on that chair, women know all too well, I got to thinking that I was just overreacting and doing too much online research! Then she came in and sure enough, the doctor did a hands-on breast exam and said she felt something, as well as noticed the visible differences between my left and right breasts. I could tell she was unhappy that I had skipped my last mammogram, but I was on FMLA and taking care of my mother in hospice. Nonetheless, I was scheduled for a mammogram and ultrasound, if necessary, per doctor's orders a few days later. Usually, I would have to wait weeks but was glad not to have to wait long to get some results. I told my sister, and she suggested it was fatty tissue, which she had on her screenings. I went to the appointment. Having had mammograms since my baseline at 35, this was the first time it hurt so badly that I cried. Then I had to step into another room and get an ultrasound because the technician said she saw something. I was asked to wait in a different room after getting dressed. I wasn't really sure what was going on, so I just sat and prayed that everything would be OK. I thought, "What was on the scan? What did they see?" That's when a Nurse Navigator came in and talked to me in her office about doctors that I might want to choose in the area. She gave me a Breast Cancer pamphlet and calendar, which should have been a big sign that I would have multiple doctor appointments soon. I was in shock. No one definitely said I had cancer, so what's going on? Before leaving the imagining center, I was allowed to see the scans and the radiologist told me that the spot on my breast was 4cm long Wow, what a Friday afternoon! I didn't want to cope with this news because I was hoping it wouldn't be what I was dreading to hear.

So, the following Tuesday, just a few days later, my gynecologist called to give me the official news that a malignancy was found and I requested her to send my scans to the newest breast surgeon in the area, who the Nurse Navigator mentioned would be easier to get an appointment with soon. I called him "Dr. Bowtie" because he always had on a bowtie with his suit. His office called on Wednesday and I had an initial consultation with him at the end of the week. That was soon for a new doctor...I wondered if had had many patients since he could schedule an appointment so soon! He didn't even get the medical report by my appointment but examined me and took my medical history, as well as family history and recommended a BRCA test. My mother had died six months earlier of Stage 4 cancer and had only had one mammogram in her early 50s, so I called aunts to get my family history. Dad's side had none, Mom's side had many—both of her living sisters had breast cancer in their 30's and 50's, but since they were currently in their 80's, it wasn't discussed with me until now.

I was working on the following Friday at school during lunchtime when the surgeon, Dr. Bowtie, called and said he needed to see me. I said it would be late because I had to stay at school for a meeting, and his response was that he "had no appointments and nothing else to do but wait for me." I was flustered that a doctor would wait for me, especially on a lovely Friday golf afternoon! I dropped my 10-year-old son off with his father at 4:30pm in the parking lot at the medical office and went to talk to the doctor. He told me the news that it was at least a stage 3 HER2+ cancer diagnosis, but he didn't like to talk in stages, just in next steps. He went over step-by-step what I would expect, however after hearing the *C* word, I couldn't tell you what he actually said because my mind scattered. I left the office at 6:00pm and called my aunt—my Godmother, crying because she had dealt with breast cancer and was like a mother to me. I didn't go home immediately because I wanted to calm myself and dry the tears before seeing my family at home. So, I drove to the nearby airport and was sitting in the cell phone lot in the driver's seat of my car in shock, disbelief, sadness, and afraid. Who gets told that they have a golf ball, marble, and gumball size tumors in their breast on a Friday afternoon? It wasn't Friday the 13th! That was not my idea of "happy hour!" My thought was, "Ok, breathe and think positive, I have to go home to my young son!" When I got home and had a bite, his dad asked what was going on because he saw where my appointment was and could tell that I had been crying after arriving home. I told him about my news through more tears and fear while sitting on the back porch. We hadn't been a couple for a while, but he reached out and held my hand to comfort. He wanted to help take care of me and our son throughout this struggle. Through sobs, I said, "OK." The next week I started getting calls after calls. My calendar was getting full both on my phone and in my journal calendar! I had appointments with the surgeon, oncologist, and radiation oncologist; appointments for MRIs, CTs, rays, bloodwork, PET scans, echocardiograms, ultrasounds, financial counselors, etc., etc. I had at least one medical appointment each week and then had to schedule surgery for a chemo port to be put in.me. Whew, May was already here! I was on a fast track ... no delaying anything!

1 Samuel 17:47 ~*And that all this assembly may know that the LORD does not deliver by sword or by spear: for the battle is the LORD's and He will give you into our hands.*

A Mother's Love

I consciously chose not to share my mammogram results with anyone until it was confirmed, and I knew what the plan of action would be for my diagnosis. My family knew that I was getting tests run and going to appointments with doctors, but I didn't share that they were for cancer. I was scared and felt that if I said something then it would be true, and I didn't want to speak words to "jinx" myself. I cried often in private. My bed pillows were probably soaked with tears and many boxes of tissues were bought! After the confirmed diagnosis of Stage IIIB-Inflammatory Breast Cancer and plan of care from Dr. Bowtie and my new oncologist, I shared it with my family, best friends, and boss, asking them to pray as this journey begins. I stopped by my father's assisted living and shared the diagnosis with him also. He hugged me and said he loved me, but even as I tried to be strong for him, we both cried. He was worried about many things but didn't share those concerns with me, just the assisted living nurse and staff, who also kept tabs on me. I think they wanted to be able to provide comfort to their residents by lessening my worries. It was easier to share this news with adults than my 5th grade son. However, I wanted to let him know what was going on with his Mom. He had just lost both of his grandmothers within the previous 12 months. My mother died from stage 4 cancer five weeks after her diagnosis, so he knew the **C** word and what it meant. I mustered up the strength when he was on the back porch with his father playing a video game one afternoon, and I asked them to stop so we could talk. I told him that all of these appointments I had been going to were with doctors because I had been diagnosed with breast cancer. I told him that I would have to get "cancer killing medicine" called chemo every three weeks for six rounds, have surgery on my breast, and radiation. His first words to me were, "Is this what Granny had?" I know at that moment he was worried about me dying... and although I was worried too, I told him how different my diagnosis was from Granny's. Hers couldn't be treated but mine could, and I was younger and would be healthier and strong enough to fight the cancer. But I also told him that I'd lose my hair, get sick, be tired, and not be able to do some of the things I had been doing with him. So, before any surgery or treatments began, we took a long weekend trip to an amusement park where we had season passes. I wanted to ride roller coasters and have fun with him before I was unable to enjoy those activities due to my condition and treatments. We made lots of memories!

I would start the treatments before school ended and was gifted the entire 5th grade serenating me at the final awards program and the staff wearing pink "Team Betsy" shirts for me. I knew that summer would bring a bald, sick, and boring Mom who couldn't do much other than go to medical appointments. I basically worked when and if I was able to, or stayed home in bed if I couldn't. He went camping with Scouts, to the pool or waterpark with others, had sleepovers at friends' houses, and took "guy" trips with his Dad. When it was time for a new school year to start, I was a "stay at home" Mom on medical leave. Unfortunately, I wasn't able to go to the Open House at school, Muffins with Mom, or any other school functions that I'd always attended with him during the previous elementary school years. He was starting middle school with all of these new experiences, including riding the bus and making new friends. I was confined to my home basically and unable to get in large crowds due to my weakened immune system. I had promised my mother before she passed away that I would take care of my father and make sure he was OK. Before my chemo, I visited him at least 2-3 days a week but after chemotherapy began, I was too sick to visit him even once a week. But just because I was sick or weak and unable to get out of the house, I still called him so he could hear my voice, and we could talk so he knew I was OK. My father's assisted living staff took good care of him and the nurse there answered many of his questions about my condition and treatment, that he didn't understand. Even though I had turned 50 and he was almost 91 years old, *a child is a child at any age*! I was trying to be a good Mom to my son; a good daughter to my father; and a good sister and friend. Those people were the ones who gave me strength to get through each day in this journey. Through Facebook, texts, emails, and phone calls I was able to receive much needed support and love as I faced this Pink Ribbon battle!

2 Corinthians 12:9 ~*But he said to me, "My grace is sufficient for you, for my power is made perfect in weakness." Therefore, I will boast all the more gladly about my weaknesses, so that Christ's power may rest on me.*

TEAM BETSY
HOLD THE ROPE

Chemotherapy Begins

In early May, my oncologist, who was informative and matter-of-factly with a caring spirit, called me in for an appointment. She provided the protocol for my cancer treatment. I wanted to wait a few more weeks until school ended, but there was urgency in her voice that delaying treatments was not an option. The nurse navigator told me that now was the time to get a wig while I still had hair, so it would resemble my current style. The lady at the wig shop was so helpful and shared her cancer fighting story with me also. We both cried and hugged. Now, I had a pink t-shirt, had my lemon drops and mints, lotion, essential oils, wig, face masks, and was ready with this suit of armor to fight the pink giant.   So, on Friday, the 13th of May, I got my first round of chemotherapy drugs. Friends who had survived their cancer battle gave me hope and my family, friends, and coworkers gave me supportive prayers, cards, and love. I sat in the chair getting my six hours of a cancer killing cocktail with company to make it through the day. A former coworker offered to meet me at the office and sat next to me sharing her first treatment to ease my worried mind. The first round wasn't so bad ...ok, we'll see what happens. On the third day after chemo, I got up and missed church on Sunday morning to get my post-treatment Neulasta shot. The nurse asked how I was feeling and at that point, so far so good! She indicated that after this treatment, the next five or six rounds will be an on-body injection, so I won't have to go back 27 hours later to get a shot in the oncologist's office. Well, the weekend had been fine, but after the Neulasta shot on that Mother's Day Sunday, my side effects began! When my son got home from a scout camping trip that weekend, ready to celebrate and share his trip, he was welcomed by a Mom who was vomiting and running to the restroom for both nausea and diarrhea. Ugh! It didn't get any better the next day! I didn't make it to work until Tuesday and still went in late; then Wednesday had to leave school early due to nausea and side effects. Friday was a scheduled follow up with my oncologist and the following Monday I'd get more blood drawn. And so *it* began, my routine every three weeks for the next 4-5 months would be chemo on Friday, wait for the self-injection shot on Saturday night to boost my white blood count, and prepare to be sick for 3-5 days. My hair started falling out after the second treatment, but I was prepared with wigs for when I went bald. My sister and her family came to visit Memorial Day weekend. I kept my hair for them so I wouldn't look too ill with it falling out, and my sister trimmed up the edges of my thinning hair. The week after they left, my head got shaved bald! Tears rolled down my cheeks and I felt embarrassed, but I was shedding hair worse than my dog! I put on a wig and worked when I could in my office; since the students were out for the summer, there were less germs to worry about. One of June's treatments made me so sick at work that a coworker had to drive me home. By July, one of my treatments made me so dehydrated because I couldn't keep anything in me which put me in the ER getting an IV. In August, the injection after my Neulasta treatment didn't work so I had to make a visit to the oncologist's office for them to check my blood.

I kept getting worse with each treatment and my blood work kept getting lower, meaning my ability to fight off infections was decreasing. I was wearing masks long before COVID, but as I have since learned they were basically for the same reasons to keep those germs away! I was weak, pale, losing some weight even with steroids, and still giving this battle my best shot! Soon, school would start again but my oncologists said that I would be unable to work with all of the germs from students and staff, so I finally had to take medical leave, and she completed the paperwork with a six-month return date. Chemo was really taking its toll on me! I was so thankful for the support I was given by friends, family, and coworkers. I kept thinking that whenever I had diarrhea or was vomiting that it was the ugly cancer leaving my body...just getting out of my system! This fight was tough!!!

Isaiah 41:10 ~*So do not fear, for I am with you; do not be dismayed, for I am your God. I will strengthen you and help you; I will uphold you with my righteous right hand.*

 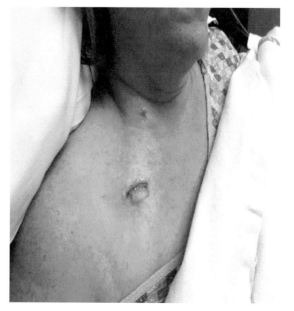

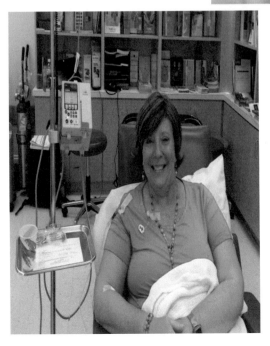

There's No Place Like Home

I worked at a school and was used to staying busy, multitasking, and usually being away from home for 10 or more hours a day. When I began my medical leave, it was strange to be home and resting during the day without it being a holiday or break. For my 50th birthday, I was given a hugger pillow to watch television shows with my feet propped up resting. I could take naps on the couch or in bed. It was like summer vacation, only extended to another season - apart from the interferences by doctor appointments, sicknesses, and general fatigue. The Patient Advocate informed me that breast cancer patients could receive four months of free house cleaning services while undergoing treatment. Those maids were a blessing to me! I didn't feel like doing any housekeeping nor did I have the energy to clean, sweep, scrub, or mop, especially in the bathroom, which needed to be sanitized before and after my chemo treatment sicknesses, *if you know what I mean.* I wanted a support group and went to a couple of different meetings, but nothing met my needs. I was either too young, too old, too far along in treatments, not finished with treatments, or whatever. Cancer affects you physically, emotionally, and spiritually but none of the groups met all three. My ambition was and is still to create a group that will provide support for other staff in the school district. I even talked to the school nurse about proposing such a group. My support came from my son and his father at home with me (and my sweet doggie). My sister called me daily to check-in. Family and friends kept in communication with me at least on a weekly basis.

When I posted on social media asking for prayers or praises, I couldn't believe how many people were showing they cared about me: childhood friends, high school and college classmates, extended family, and local friends or coworkers. I tried to keep and stay optimistic during this trial and share my status. When comments were made that I looked good... all I could say in response was that a *wig, makeup, and a smile* can do wonders! Looks may be deceiving but I knew I had to stay positive in order to get a positive outcome. Those interactions were all I could have from home, so I treasured them!

The holidays presented a new outlook as treatments continued. I wasn't feeling good for Halloween but did my best to walk around the neighborhood (well, just my street) while my son went Trick or Treating before his Dad came to take him out. By Thanksgiving, everyone knew I wasn't cooking and a hermit who needed to get out of the house. I was able go out to a restaurant and enjoy a meal with my family, father, and in-laws at the beach. Almost all of my Christmas shopping was done online since I was now a homebody who was unable to get out and go while on daily radiation treatments. Never before had I taken advantage of Cyber Monday, but I wasn't allowed to go out and had no energy to shop anyway! My son and I took two weekend get-aways to visit an aunt and my sister in their homes. I was exhausted before I left and after I returned but needed to do what I could while I felt like I could. Home had been my sanctuary and battle ground.

Joshua 1:9 ~*Have I not commanded you? Be strong and courageous. Do not be afraid; do not be discouraged, for the LORD your God will be with you wherever you go.*

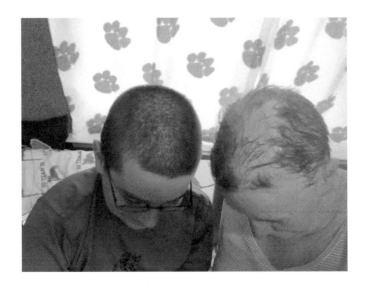

Stormy Surgery

Chemo ended finally and after a couple of weeks, I met with a new surgeon to plan for my mastectomy. Although I wasn't looking forward to it, I had been told from the beginning that I would need to have my left breast removed and could elect to have a double mastectomy and reconstruction. Of course, recovery is harder...plastic surgery after radiation is complicated and it would require more surgeries...obviously, I was ready to opt for the single mastectomy. My original oncology surgeon, Dr. Bowtie, had moved to another state to practice, so I went to a local surgeon near my oncologist's office. We discussed the mastectomy procedure and all of its problems and side effects. I got teary eyed thinking about more changes, until she mentioned that I could be a candidate for a partial mastectomy. She would just remove the remaining tumors and lymph nodes under my arm that were affected by the cancer... 1 golf ball size, 2 marbles, and 2 gumballs were shrunk by chemotherapy. I was sent to a physical therapist in anticipation of lymphedema. My sister drove up to go with me as I was fitted, and we both ordered sleeves for me to wear after the surgery [one beige and the other black]. However, a hurricane came to our area a week before surgery, and she went home. I was worried that there would be a delay because of the power outages...well, the date of the surgery stayed the same but due to issues at the hospital with closings and evacuations in the beach area, my time of surgery went from 7:30am to 11:00am to 3:30pm. I had not eaten anything since 8:00pm the night before. We had to make plans for my son's grandfather to be at the house to pick him up since we wouldn't be home in time after school to let him in or feed him.

Months ago, my port surgery's anesthesia made me wake up thinking I couldn't breathe, and sure enough the partial mastectomy / lumpectomy's anesthesia made me wake up thinking that I was lost under the covers and thinking no one could find me. Apparently, I make a funny post-op patient! I remember the pain after both surgeries and thankfully they are just memories which I don't want to relive. I left the hospital wearing a supportive tube top for a couple of days post-surgery and not showering. When I first saw the wound on my body, I teared up. But I had a resemblance of a breast left, unlike other patients who may not have had anything there. My follow up appointment with the surgeon indicated that the lumpectomy was a success... cancer cells were removed! I was one happy girl who was rocking the pink and sharing the news with friends and family. Lymphedema caused some issues afterwards; and future attempts to have my blood pressure or lab work taken will be on the opposite arm, but that's minor compared to what it could have been. I can't begin to tell you how many people prayed for me, cared about me, and shared their love and positive thoughts with me **during this battle.**

James 5:14 *~Is anyone among you sick? Let them call the elders of the church to pray over them and anoint them with oil in the name of the Lord.*

Radiation Repair

After wearing the elastic tube top to support the surgery area for three weeks, it was time to schedule an appointment with the radiation oncologist. The office squeezed me in for what I thought was a consultation but was actually for them to take more x-rays and scans, prior to the radiation. Radiation wouldn't start until after the doctor could review and plan my new radiation treatment schedule. Well, a few days later, that office calls and I'm scheduled for my first treatment on the Sunday before Thanksgiving. At the initial treatment, I was given my calendar with 7 weeks of appointments. Originally, they were mostly at 1:15pm and then later had to be changed when my father also needed to have radiation treatments for 3 weeks, so we were given back-to-back appointment times. Within the first ten days of radiation, the skin from my neck to under my arm and breast was pink. I faithfully used the special lotion they gave me as well as radiation deodorant and soap to keep my skin healthy for radiation treatments. My father never had those setbacks from his radiation for skin cancer. But during the next ten days, my skin started itching and peeling like a bad sunburn! Soon I started getting third degree burns that hurt badly and I had to use prescription cream that fire-burn victims are given. I remember smelling fried chicken and no one was in the kitchen cooking, but it was actually my skin scorching from the burn machine that I was smelling. I was frying from the inside, and hopefully the radiation was killing what cancer may be left in me. I took a picture of my burned and purple peeling chest...but it was only on the left side, the right was still dewy white freckled flesh. Those weeks were painful in the healing process and there was nothing else to do but use the cream and suffer through the pain. What a difference that radiation triangle made on my appearance! Well, the next phase of radiation was called the "Boost" because it had to go through my left breast and I guess, needed an extra boost to get inside. Those final ten days gave my charred area time to heal. I continued using the non-aluminum deodorant and soap, special aloe lotion, and burn cream as the radiation oncologist and technicians told me to. If nothing else, I did what all of my doctors said but prayed to the Great Physician for healing also. He fought this battle too!

Matthew 19:26 ~*With God all things are possible.*

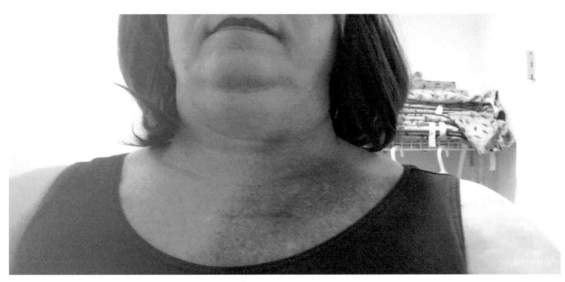

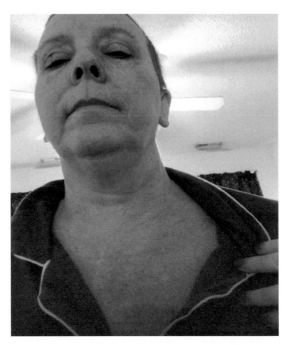

Moving On

       Chemo complete, surgery complete, radiation complete.... What's next? After letting my body have a couple of weeks to recover, I thought I was ready, and it was time to return to work. I had already reduced my hours for the initial 10 weeks during the summer, and then taken leave for over five months during the school year. I wasn't sick anymore, but I felt like I needed to be back at work doing what I'd always done and work at the school since boredom was setting in on me. My radiation surgeon released me to work part-time for the first week and full-time for the next. I was excited! After my first day of working only 4 hours, I came home and slept for 3 hours to recover. I was exhausted, but also hadn't worked in a while. Tuesday came and I had to get my usual three-week Herceptin dosage. The oncologist asked if I had returned to work, and I told her part-time and then full-time next week. She looked at me with concerned eyes and asked how it was going. I told her that I was worn out but had only started working the day before. She said that I needed to give my body time to recover and take 2-3 more weeks at part-time before going full-time. According to her, my body needed as much time to heal as it had to be treated, but I didn't have time to take off for another six months! My sick days were coming to an end, and I was concerned about losing pay. I still had medical bills and a mortgage to pay. So, I went to work that afternoon and the next morning, just trying to see how I could manage the fatigue. By Thursday, it was evident that the doctor knew best, and I needed to give myself more time to rest. I let my principal know Friday morning that I would need to take a couple more weeks at part-time hours before returning... not what either of us wanted, but probably what we both knew was needed for my health to improve. She was just glad that I could return and assist her at school with administrative duties for a few hours. I would continue the three-week Herceptin doses until May while taking Tamoxifen daily for the next 5 years. I had mammograms scheduled on my left breast every six months, and the right breast annually for 3 years and then both yearly after that mark, provided nothing recurs. I realized I will have echocardiograms, MRIs, bone density tests, CT scans, and lots of doctor visits for the foreseeable future! But I have faith that God has a plan for me, and this was part of Him showing me that my health needs to be a priority; and my family and friends are close at heart even if some live far away. There have been friends and coworkers who followed my progress and provided more support and encouragement than I ever thought I'd get. I'm taking it easy and feel like it's time to move on.

Jeremiah 29:11 ~*For I know the plans I have for you," declares the LORD, "plans to prosper you and not to harm you, plans to give you hope and a future."*

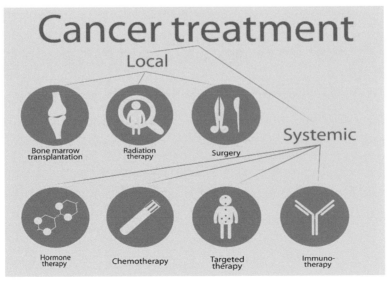

The Five-Year Plan(s)

- Part One:

I continued to see my oncologist regularly--going from every three weeks to every six weeks to eventually every three months and then every six months. My bloodwork still had some issues that required monitoring, but I was steadily getting the release from their watchful eyes. I had mammograms scheduled for a bilateral every year and a diagnostic every six months. Due to the medication prescribed, I could have complications with my bones, so I also had bone scans and bone density tests at appropriate intervals. I had episodes of falling and imbalance that caused me to have to see the primary care and have additional tests prepared. I regained my weight and then tried losing it with different diets, but still didn't have the energy to get up and move to lose the extra pounds. I was given the opportunity to take a six-week LIVESTRONG program at the local YMCA to facilitate giving me a jump start. I participated each week but when the time came to an end, I didn't see me continuing the program. It was a great experience to be part of this training with other cancer survivors. I would recommend others to at least give it a chance if selected for the course. With the responsibilities in my school administration job, taking care of my elderly father, keeping house for my family, preparing meals, and most importantly giving my now pre-teenage son time and attention needed, my life was already busy enough and I couldn't add more to my already full plate of things to do. I feel that during this period of time, I needed the companionship of coworkers, family, and friends to keep me going. I was tired of being isolated from others. And I was getting used to the new me with scars, aches, pains, and memories holding me together. It was a time of growing, stressing, and changing—but I couldn't add more to my days, weeks, months, or years to my life. A change of jobs and retirement would be in my future, and I was ready to take that punch!

Matthew 6:27 ~And who of you by being worried can add a single hour to his life?

- Part Two:

Close to my five-year mark, I noticed a lump on my right breast that I would mention to my oncologist at the upcoming office visit in a few weeks. The PA saw me for that follow up appointment. It was the first time that I had been seen by her, so she did the general overview and history questions as expected for the "get to know you" appointment. However, when I shared the information about the spot on the other breast and how it was tender to touch, she immediately took action. This was during the COVID-19 pandemic era of 2021 and actual "hands on touching" was not the norm anymore, but she did feel the lump and scheduled a biopsy for me. She also told me not to wait for an appointment but call right away if I found something again. Needless to say, I left upset due to her urgent concern, but also content knowing that it would be treated and hopefully it was caught early. The medical staff constantly showed how much they cared for me and other patients. I recommended my oncologist to anyone who shared they needed one. The biopsy was scheduled about a week after that appointment and my oncologist called to report that there were no cancer cells found. Whew....what a blessing that message was! My next mammogram had already been scheduled and they would follow up in another three months. However, just after Christmas 2021, I had a call from my favorite oncologist that the Breast Cancer Index (BRCA) five-year testing results came back, and unfortunately, I would need to stay on the hormone blocking therapy for another five years. I still have that message saved in my phone voicemail. Most cancer survivors stop taking adjuvant aromatase-inhibitors after five years, but I needed more time based on the BRCA results. Anastrozole reduces the risk of breast cancer by 53% after 7 years of follow-up treatment and 50% after 10.9 years of follow-up treatment according to a study from Drugs.com. It was sad to think that I may have to fight this *Pink Giant* again; and wondered if I'd have the will power to go through chemotherapy, radiation, surgery, and all the treatments once more. I decided not to dwell on what could be but rather what is now—so that's my story for 5 more years. During a severe weather "no school" day, I woke up with a stuff nose and took a cold pill. I ended up getting choked so much that my son had to call 911. It was a horrible experience, but I thought it was a one-time thing because the gel pill got stuck. Nope, now anytime I was taking my prescriptions, I got choked or felt like the medicine was getting lodged in my throat. Now what?

A few weeks later, I saw my oncology PA and told her about my choking episodes and asked if it could be related to radiation burns affecting my esophagus. She indicated that I needed to see my primary care physician immediately, so the oncology office called over, and I saw my primary doctor the next day. I told her that I was worried that the radiation therapy had damaged my esophagus, but my primary care doctor assured me that it would have affected me sooner rather than 5 years later. I was scheduled for an endoscopy with my gastroenterologist, and she found that my esophagus had stricture. A normal esophagus is about 20mm in diameter and mine was less than 8mm at one point because her tool was 9mm and she had to scrape to get through to the stomach. Another upper endoscopy called an esophageal dilation was scheduled to stretch my esophagus due to the dysphagia. The gastroenterologist was able to expand my esophagus to 12-15mm which was better for me to swallow. I began taking medication for acid reflux and didn't have any more episodes of choking for more than a year. After the first choke post-stretching, I scheduled an appointment for another dilation. Cancer is scary but choking is scarier!!! I ordered from Amazon.com a "De-Choker" which resembled a toilet plunger to cover my mouth for use in instances of choking. It was only used once but that was enough to not want to have to use it again! Hopefully at the 10-year mark, I will be able to tell the Part 3 version of this battle!

2 Timothy 2:3-4 ~*Share in suffering as a good soldier of Christ Jesus. No soldier gets entangled in civilian pursuits, since his aim is to please the one who enlisted him.*

Spreading My Story

I didn't share my story immediately because I thought that it was vainful of me to write about my experiences and think others would be interested. Then one day, a friend of mine shared with me that her 23-year-old special needs daughter had been diagnosed with breast cancer. That hit a nerve more than I realized!!! It was hard enough for me as a mature, five decades-old woman to go through the trauma of biopsies, appointments, treatment, side-effects, and life with an aggressive Stage IIIB Inflammatory Breast Cancer diagnosis; but now this "child" and her mother, aunt, grandmother, and family would also have to endure that battle. I felt a need to expose my struggles and spiritual strength again to others. Fighting this *Pink Giant* is a tough pill to swallow (no pun intended, well maybe). I wish that chemo, radiation, surgery, pills, and side effects weren't part of the battle so many people face when dealing with cancer of any kind! I cried when a male friend of mine found a lump on his breast and told me that he would have a mammogram like I did and asked me about what I went through so he would know what to expect. It hurt every time a cousin of mine sent a picture and I knew she was wearing a wig or sent a text about her cancer plan. Cancer sucks but it is part of this world, so we as members of this world have to put up with evils thanks to the original sinners, Adam and Eve. Recently, I was asked to participate in a Community Oncology Alliance summit on Capitol Hill. What an honor to speak as an advocate and cancer survivor in hopes of getting more support for independent Oncology offices with congressmen and representatives! I chose to receive treatment locally rather than going to the Medical University because I knew chemotherapy would take its toll and cause me to get sick, plus I didn't want to have to deal with a hotel or patient housing in a strange bed or bathroom two hours from where I live. I wanted the comfort of being close to my doctor's office, being at home, and with people who loved me. One day, we can only hope to see and be part of a holy and healthy kingdom of God...so that's why I'm spreading my story and sharing my trials and tribulations for anyone who may be interested in reading what to expect or remembering what they went through from my recollections of fighting this Pink Giant!

Romans 10:15 *~And how are they to preach unless they are sent? As it is written, "How beautiful are the feet of those who preach the good news!"*

Many thanks to all of my family and friends,
Dr. Touloukian, Dr. Parnell, Dr. Bowtie (Croshaw), PA Tonya,
RN Ashley, Pharmacist Erick, RN Gabby, CMC Breast
Health Navigator Jeanne, Coastal Cancer Center, Homewood Elementary
School, P.E.O. Chapter S, COA/CPAN, and
my dog, Sierra, for helping me fight this battle!

Fighting the Pink Giant

Made in the USA
Columbia, SC
26 October 2024

44633604R00015